antibody

//

BOOKS BY REBECCA SALAZAR

sulphurtongue

antibody

poems

REBECCA SALAZAR

McClelland & Stewart

McClelland & Stewart and colophon are registered trademarks of
Penguin Random House Canada Limited.

The authorized representative in the EU for product safety and compliance is
Penguin Random House Ireland, Morrison Chambers, 32 Nassau Street,
Dublin D02 YH68, Ireland, https://eu-contact.penguin.ie

Published simultaneously in the United States of America.

Library and Archives Canada Cataloguing in Publication data
is available upon request.

ISBN: 978-0-7710-2047-6
ebook ISBN: 978-0-7710-2048-3

Cover design by Talia Abramson
Cover images: (snake) Ophidii Tab. 3 from Fauna japonica (1838) / Biodiversity
Heritage Library via Flickr; (bird) illustration by Talia Abramson, based on an
image by Lasse Nystedt / Unsplash; (mouse) illustration by Talia Abramson,
based on an image by creativenature.nl / Adobe Stock

Typeset in Portrait Text by Sean Tai
Printed in Canada

McClelland & Stewart
A division of Penguin Random House Canada
320 Front Street West, Suite 1400
Toronto, Ontario, M5V 3B6, Canada

penguinrandomhouse.ca

1 2 3 4 5   29 28 27 26 25

Penguin
Random House
McCLELLAND & STEWART

None of these things exist. You have no reason to believe me.

—*Carmen Maria Machado,* In the Dream House

CONTENTS

// infect //

// sever //

DEDICATION // TRIGGER WARNING

For the many-gendered kin who are forced to be evidence,
and for the stories we could tell, given our tongues.

To fellow survivors, this offering: these poems relive in graphic detail
the experience of sexual violence, silencing, pregnancy loss,
chronic illness, and suicidality. What matters more than this book
is your consent, your agency in choosing whether or how much of it
you read. If this is as far as you read, thank you.

This book is still written for you.

antibody

//

// infect //

WITCH HUNT

too many wannabe crowleys
con our teeth from us for pleasure,
stir our cauldrons counterclockwise
on the wrong stroke with their bent cocks.
remember when they scorned us as faddish,
trend-witches, all while whipping out
their wands for instagram? remember
when they blamed us for the limpness
of their lyrics, beat our bodies, stole
the markings they left, and passed these
off as newfound runes? my warlock

gaslights me for breakfast. poisons me,
then vomits in my lap and plays at victim.
my pain is really his is all my fault is just
a curse he has to bear. he dolls me up,
one hand shoved up my ass not quite
without consent, to puppet at my mouth
and make the world watch me say *papa*
is a good ventriloquist. he calls this hoo-
doo, like his white skin knew dark magic
only as a sonic boon to juice for praise
from other fools. he only asks forgiveness
for his mental illness causing him
to cause my mental illness, which is less real
than his own. he says he needs my wisdom
teeth for spellcraft, but the spell is one
to cast my words against women like us.

let's watch him claim this is a witch hunt,
like the rest. let's be the bitch cunts
he regrets, as though we women never
once were burned when forced to stoke
the flames for our own funerals. as though
we witches cannot hunt where we were hunted.

TWO OF SWORDS

unwoman across airport bench / pinned
by cartoon hypodermic needles
(not the safest lumbar puncture)

two of swords / a sabre through the shoulders
and another through the ribs / adverse blades
extract the flashback, crack scar tissue,
and that past year slicks the floor

two of swords / departure gate
remember when he left you here
skirting the issue he forced up
in you / his promise soon to visit (judas kiss)

he kept you hungry, made a hollow
in your belly he could worship, spit
a child in / the more he extracted
the thinner and sharper he grew

two of swords / a local anesthetic
long sharp vacuum, dilation
& curettage (spoon in the gut)

airport lounge, body reclined
shaking knees / eyes sewn open
two clocks winding forward and back

//

ptsd is a physical fiend
ptsd is a bodily bind

limbs alchemized to lead,
catatonia (hypoarousal)
the diaphragm halts / lungs
exhale, power down

paging passenger x
paging passenger ex

(it's a joke)

is the body a vessel for spit
is the pelvis a cockpit to fill

count the passengers
the belly's forced to carry

prepare for descent
from the ceiling / the ghost
of a sword on a string overhead

suit of cups / fragile baggage
that cracks from the fall / oozes
evidence to slick the thighs, remember
orange dress to skirt the issue

two of swords / airport toilet stall
remember how you flushed
your public shame
and all forensic proof

your perjury

(collect yourself)

DIRT ENGINE

stirring sand with dry hands
three crones cast runes
of bed death and desire,
dust-etch auguries: nine years
of fallowness, unfeeling hours,
a smoking sun, unfinished child
unliving in the gut—
                blood tide.

the witches' bent hands scatter omens,
lost teeth in the wind. each grain of ash
a future unbecoming as it drifts
and births a thousand sickly stars

DUENDE

when i begin to lose my knives   and memories
abuelo tells me i have come of age   and woken it.

     most spirits in our family make unrelenting thieves.

my duende steals my baking tins, my winters.
it remembers once cajoling me to trudge hip-deep
in howling snow to land my hips   on men, across town—
     this, while men cast bones to ask the blizzard
what to sink in me: their cocks   their unborn children   or an axe.
my duende steals my winters since it watched men strip,   unzip
my parka and attempt to sink   all three.

my knives, it takes to stop me cutting
out more time   the blank hours
when I disappear,   returning minus limbs,
my hollowed joints crying their loss,
and so my duende gleans   new legs and arms,
who knows from where.

my duende steals my baking tins
after i dream i helped men set a cooking fire,
only to smell smoke   find men gone
                and find a baby   charred fast
                in a casserole dish

my duende guides me to forget   fullness,
the child's burnt smell that fed and made me ill.

abuelo says our loss is generations
preordained.   my duende hides my cut marks
with a latent rash of cradle cap.

          my duende steals my memory
of the child's face,   spares me remembering
if i know her parentage,   spares me remembering if underneath
that blizzard shroud men made me

                              hers.

RAPE KIT

i.

if there is tenderness
there may be tension

if there is swelling, pain,
contain thy filthy self

ii.

if the paper gown covers

if the legs slant inwards
from the stirrups, knees
meet like wind-felled trees

if there is any chance
of pregnancy if there is
any chance of pregnancy

if the doctor says the speculum
is smaller than the average cock

if the doctor rubs the speculum
to warm it in gloved hands

if you consent

if the flesh could meld
to cold steel

iii.

if the paper gown covers
are you covered?

if necessary, ask me to repeat

if there is pre-existing trauma

          turn back
if there is a trauma
          turn back

if the body could close
its accesses at will

if there is tenderness
          turn back

iv.

raw cunt,
cover thyself

v.

if not covered for bloodwork,
split a lip between the teeth,
make of its bracing salt
an offering

vi.

if seeking salve
you are   turned back

if pain or infection recurs
scrape it out,
cleanse the too-porous self

if there is pain
it is symptom
of purity

UNICORNS

you keep your unicorns
as bookends, paperweights,
display their frozen gorgeousness
to woo impressionable foals.
you probe our hindquarters
for suppleness and youth.
you make an impression.

i was unsuitable, as ingenue:
too sickly to be fresh-faced
with my fever fug and bald spots.
not doe-eyed. not horny enough.

you rode me and my will
to the ground, spurned me
with scars, carving
your spurs into my flanks.
you un-stabled me:
one more depressive
pixie dream horse
for the gallery of whores
you keep in irons in the barn.

suitably drawn and quartered,
i was only a surrogate virgin,
a lure for more mystical beasts.

break into the flooded school tonight
in skintight latex, rubber boots. let's play
apocalypse against the rusted lockers
of our youth—carve mix & match initials
in the rust, wade into classrooms ankle-deep
& bend a body rough over upended desks,
make waves.
          let's pass a bottle of cheap gin
until it's empty, spin to reshuffle pairs,
go deeper. sequins in torchlight
down the hall, splashing staccato
under flooded stairs. M ties a silk scarf,
binds our wrists, leads my abandon
into dark, metallic water at our knees
through ruined basement labs, lush
laughter of our other lovers echoing
above, gasp of mirth, she swings me
breathless to the wall, sinks facedeep
in my skirt, her long hair spidering
the surface of the flood,
                  follow the ripples
of her movement as we drift, bounce
back against some corner voyeur—
one of ours?—not so, this low-light
yellow glow, dim flood-length oilskin
not the dresscode for our fete—our friends
upstairs have faces—
            hell catches
my throat. my untied hand clenches
M's shoulder and she rises, wet skin
cooling as she rises taller than herself,
pulled upwards as by meathooks
in her back, water sluicing her hair,

our bound hands drag. suspend us,
aching chandelier—
                    oilskin watcher
glides toward us, long neck stretching
out of sight, faceless and unmoved
as my grip fails, wet silk cuts bloodflow
as we levitate, M's face a silent
open sleep, eyes clouded white,
my shoulder pops—
                    above us,
fine static, night broken by hailstones
the size of our fists.

THE MISSIONARY POSITION

tells you it's no voluntourist,
just wants to flash
god-light and orphan-hug
selfies abroad.
it's slow-fooding
a fast one over you,
ramshackling a clapboard
chapel on your last arable land.

i'm getting close to mother nature.
that's her on the mixed-salad package,
with photoshopped kale laced
to veil her waxed bosom.
she peels back my husk
with her teeth.

ask which one of us
brings home the pants,
which wears the meat.
ask what's on second,
who's the top.

at the bibles for missions
art clearance, a buff-chested swan
mounts a needlepoint leda,
the greenery cross-
stitched to bind her.

you can't make heads or tails
without a phallus in the cut.

we all know finding god
is penetration from above.

TO BAIT FISH WITHAL

i teach survival skills
since those who cannot do
teach
           eleven yrs old
in manhattan and vying for sex
since i learned girlhood early
and this was that good shit—
stuck in turnpike traffic
puking in a plastic bag
the splatter on my pants
wrong kind of wet
between the legs
—when i thought men
liked dirty girls

           remember
this in twenty years, same
colour vomit flecks my jeans
upon confessing how i want
to die
           this world
annihilating people every day
who look increasingly like me
—like i needed convincing

//

my carcass a sensorium for danger
cuerpo seco
teachable moment

call this living if you will, but
self-annihilation
                 is the subtlest
& least visible of arts
                       strategic etch
of skin picked off in rashers
trichotillomania
the expert creditor
excoriates a pound of flesh
in artful scrapings
not a jot of blood

//

i teach you how not to do

do not   develop c-cups
when nobody wants a titted
kindergartner
                least of all
the kid

do not   dissociate at parties
when the local rape apologist
entwines around you from behind
beard scratching at your bra

do not   re-mortify the flesh
fingernails scarring each seam
unstitching each tissue

do not   exact his price
upon yourself,
             cheap flesh

do not   decant the bile
they raise in you upon yourself

do not   spill over
and over to overcome living

TRUE

because the hell you gave me bore no name
when it was given i have learned what it is called
in true crime podcasts   plaster bust casts
of manson and bundy   i learn your genus fingering
your outline in the specimens of killers
hear your cadence in interrogation tapes   i study
their techniques to read in retrospect how you
groomed me
                                        and who knew healing
looked like googling crime scene photos to remake
my chalk dimensions   bust   waist   hips
                                                        recalibrate
my memory to fit this profile   step one love-bomb
step two gaslight step three nitpick step four blame
shift step five break down step six death threat step six death
threat step six death threat
                                        lucky thing
you had a penchant for my birthdate   number of the beast
i cannot guess how long you wanted me
                                                        alive

explosive narcissist stoking flammable girls
this is your era   isn't it
ted bundy was named heartthrob of the week
i'm sure you're next
                                        oh true love
when the serials lose count and when the zodiac
shifts into retrograde   solve this   for me

CANON

my face launches a thousand
lawsuits for harassment,
but sweetie, you need me;
just look at your line breaks.
allow me to edit your
unasked consent, break
your imagined hymen over
quibbles about hyphens;
not born yesterday, you're
younger than my first book,
but lolita, you're no kid,
no kid could write this new,
could come the way you do.
I'll ejaculate over your body
of work. don't go feeling
embattled. everyone knows
cannons   canons
are surrogate cocks; stroke
the gun, or get fucked.
darling, art's a dirty job
but someone's gotta do me.

EXQUISITE CORPSE

after Nicole Sealey

i think my voice is being ripped from me—

worry tastes so dirty when it's spread out like a banquet.

i am terrified i built my poetry on the backs of violent men.

when brown women die who specifically is responsible for the
eroticization of our deaths?

we are in waiting rooms to report our own drowning.

come, the algae blooms are so thick, we can walk on water we can't drink,

thick with seductive coloratura—

put my body on the block and blow me like a reed—

i'll miss you most when they kill us,

and millions of bacteria love you,

sitting like cats on whatever hurts most.

//

it makes your grief sit down, this house. it makes you chairs when you need
   justice.

when it's our turn we only hope for whole joints, impassioned graffiti.

we are told to treat texts as separate from people,

to cauterize each wound to prevent our dreams from regrowing.

someone teach me otherwise.

i tell you i want to be new, undo myself differently this time.

i'm summoning my future body

but the body (little bitch) won't love you back.

tell them the body is a blade that sharpens by cutting,

nothing could be easier, but first you must overcome that cold carcass:

animal skinning itself in reverse & sewing itself up wrong,

born to be reassembled later by some other might.

//

i can't take back this skin.

i have praised your god for the blessing of the body, snuck from pleasure
  to pleasure, lying for it.

how to demote god to the middle of the paragraph?

make no mistake, i wanted to kneel before you. make the glass shake,

pluck the sun out like an eye and eat my share of meat in the dark—

finally, a sin worth hurting for, a fervour, a sweet—

yes, the body has more choices than it knows.

every tooth-filled thing opens its mouth & the whole night howls.

SLAPP / article i

SLAPPs [Strategic Lawsuits Against Public Participation]
are lawsuits, or the threat of a lawsuit, directed against
individuals or organizations, in order to silence and
deter their public criticisms and advocacy for change.
—*Canadian Civil Liberties Association*

did justice consent to her blindfold
or tie it herself　　　　　little slut
█████████████　　　asking for it
in every court house

count at least one
of each
in every room:
　　　　　　　a) a ██████ white man carrying a weapon & a grudge
　　　　　　　b) a rapist gathering your public body

██ you are ████　　　never yours
but a rentable target for buckshot or death

look away for the ████████████
for the impact

the sting of a SLAPP in a knife fight

what good is a ███████ defense
when its subject is already harmed
beyond action
　　　　　　　too little
　　　　　　　too legal
　　　　　　　too late

the only succour offered to the ██████████ silenced
is the chance to cut our own tongues
before others cut them from us

to display　　　as proof
　　　　　　as legal precedence
　　　　　　as slander
　　　　　　as a ██████████

31

// sever //

CARBON FOOTPRINT OF ONE (1) RAPE

flushed condom, pipe damage. later, emissions repairing, the travel for parts.
foil condom wrapper garbage-fished, perused for pinpricks (saved as evidence).

water to wash hands.
water to wash the stained sheets.
water to wash the imprints from the body.
water to wash the imprints from the body.

emissions: cab ride far away across the city.
trash meal in a gas station: plastic bottle, foil chip bag.
fear pheromones in the park—flora, fauna detecting.

the blank hours (how many lost).

//

plastic pregnancy test, cellophane and cardboard package.
water to wash hands.
the blank hours (water left running).

the attempts.
pills bought, ingested, vomited in waterways.

emissions moving to a home unhaunted.
moving boxes.
carbon burn of the letters, the books.

water to wash the imprints from the body.
water just to hear it run, forgetting.

emissions: traffic-stunted cab ride to the ER, ambulance too pricey.
rayon, cotton, plastic, paper: menstrual pads bled through and clothing ruined.
rayon, cotton, plastic, paper: multiply these (who could diva cup miscarried
    blood).
plastic hospital wristbands.
dilation and curettage.
metal speculum wrenched out of shape (the clench).
carbon emissions of the hospital incinerator.

the blank hours (a death of a kind).

how many solvents, how much bleach to sterilize the hospital, its instruments
    per patient.
how much water to scrub practised hands.

//

prescription pads depleted and wastebasket-tossed.
blister pack plastic and foil.

plastic pharmacy jars.

plastic pharmacy jars.

plastic pharmacy jars.

carbon footprint of the psychopharmacology that keeps suicide at bay.
residual contaminants leached into waterways from human urine.
SSRIs metabolized.
flora and fauna medicated, sans consent, from effluent.

how many years of this.

//

if a person was disposable, how many.
if a person is disposable, what else.

//

human essentialism (he said you were special).

illusions of being more than mineral, than filth.
failure to feel equal to an instrument, a single-use.

cost of unasked consent.
cost of
cost of

cost of boundaries that separate a body from the earth.
carbon footprint of what elevates us to the dignity of men.

ANAPHYLAXIS

tell me i'm overreacting.
                          this body refuses
to breathe air with yours, to be co-formed
by viral load   by matter you would share

                          lungs clutch
                          guts clench

survivor flesh rejects a world
that will not let it live
                          what can the gut derive
from whiteness and abuse
                          we shit it out
before it touches us   again
                          again   again

we cough and splutter   choke on *back to normal*
spit   co-morbid lives

& now   all fibers of my being
inflame   refuse assimilating proteins

begging, *put me out of being*

hypothesis:
          the food you eat the air you breathe
          are trying to eat you back

hypothesis:
          wake every morning in a chronic knot
          as every organ self-destructs
          as every tendon twangs to keep the self together

antithesis:
  the violators grasp
  to claim a sickly morsel   hunters' trophy

this body is allergic to your world
and i am starving
    for connection
that will not assimilate
  my cells   my will

tattoo this spell in epi-pen & pfizer on my seizing thigh:

mask up fight MAiD
   & each new genocide machine

    fuck every rapist's new reunion tour
    fuck every rape joke calling us the groomers

listen:

when we ask for access

    do not give us death
       for your convenience

when we ask for   masks on
                    no police

                  no new reasons to die

i dare you
              tell me i overreact

as my skin blooms with hives.

                        & just try

to shove your matter
down this swollen throat.

INCUBUS

old hag & her night mare are snared
in the low-drooping arch of my eyelid.
she knows better. only ponies
trundle low enough (shag bellies
brushing burrs and earth)
to ride through the eye
of my needling gaze.

you were hag-like,
riding me. like her,
you'd not get off
your high horse,
never asked
to gain admittance,

claimed hunters hold licence
to prey upon sleepers, and entered.

//

go on,
old goon.

hack off
my hands
for hag-bait,
trail blood
down my stumps.

//

now, when i sleep, i sleep like demons
come for me: hard heart a-canter,
nagging jugular, arms pinned as though
by leaden pitchforks weltering my wingspan.

white nights, i'm striking eyelashes for match-light,
itching to burn your afterimage from my insides.

wake me, i dare you. watch me wax ravenous
as hot slivers of moon, and watch me wolf down,
guzzling the dark to staunch the ache.

//

when you foamed me at the mouths
and left me feral to the woods,
you split my hydra tongue to shreds.

we'll multiply what you cut off.

we'll weave a tapestry
of cries binding your name.

OILSPILL

i name _____ and the world ends.
run. stop writing & live in margins.
never settle longer than a day, carry no comforts.

a librarian hides me in bookstacks one night,
requests i pay them by removing
all the rapists from the bookshelves.
in the morning my hands burn,
the bookstacks so lightened they float.

outside the campus town, an alto singer
code-sings of a safe house by the sea
where she & other tongue-cut birds keep
one another. once arrived, i meet three girls
whose sister has gone missing in the sea.

we wade apocalyptic waters, skirt sinkholes
that yawn to consume us, but our trials
taught us well to mince steps, locate drag marks
of a body pulled below; we dig, stirring murk
to unbury two hands we then grasp to pull free,
feel opposing force pulling her back below sea—

hours of plying salt water and we birth her back
to shore, her naked legs necrotic with black welts
from zip-tie bounds, her lungs expelling bitumen
to breathe. under a red and sable sky, the ocean stirs

as crude white tentacles of every violation we have fled
rise from the water, blotting out the sun to tower
over us and churn the beach into a tailings pond,
a petri dish where we, the specimens, are pinned.

DISSOCIATIVE LOOP

pretty tiring some days,

pulling threads so devoutly.

purled linoleum skitters: dropped

pills tessellate swirling dust.

petrified tea stains & dry,

perspiration-tinged soy dregs.

parched throat, soiled dishes,

past tyrannies simmering dirges

—ply that sweet dissociation.

pause the swollen drowse,

peel tight skin downwards:

pallid, tortuous swan dive.

pray this suicide disease

proceeds through small deaths:

phantom teeth & soft drownings.

pretend to sleep, dream.

the (w)elder left inheritance:
a box of cracked steel rings,
some charred with curses
they absorbed. mi madre's
childhood armour. in metal
bubbled black or clean-cracked
is a legacy of harms undone.
was it protective, keeping
broken rings? the archive
of a life preserved with simple
ornaments, a father's spell.

mi madre and i neglect signs.
we two are excellent forgetters.
madre lost three emeralds
from a gold ring when they shrunk
and slipped their bindings.
that winter, i destroyed
organic loops: one fragile shell,
one fireproof black coral, both
flaking to ash in sweaty palms;
one amber signet chipped
by tooth marks i could not identify.

madre and i clutter our hands
with these makeshift defenders.
what harms they deflect we forget
how to see; our (w)elder never
passed his magics down, left
daughters and granddaughters
imitating gestures, circling
a flame with glittered hands
that cannot feel its warmth.

48

we are protectors binding
harms we cannot name
with any ligament we find.
madre's witch finger: cut-
taut tendon holds the crook,
a spring wound up with history.
my time travel: brain coiled
in trauma loops, repeating
cycles in the dark to reach
before the (w)elder's death,
return his breath, invert our loss.

POEM FOR UNWILLING MOTHERS

embroider white cushions
with nests of hair pulled
from the semen-clogged drain.

stain the mattress every cycle.
new blood pools new relief
maps: a lunar topography
outlines still-nameless craters.

the ragged spaces in this poem
silhouette you dangling
a newborn aloft by the ankle.

it spells an anagram of every name
you've chalked across the floor
to summon daughters you won't have.

it nuzzles your breast, raising
delicate folds like the scalded milk-skin
you'll dissect with the blade
of a spoon.

it asks if you can hear the ticking.

it will birth itself, choking
and noosed with wet cords,
a stray spool-shuttle snared in the loom.

wrap knots of bloodroot
in this page. steep this pessary
in swamp water to staunch
newly scraped wombs.

re-engineer the cogs burst
from your biological clock
into a pipe bomb,

and smudge your face while burying
this poem in that ravine
where tiny skeletons are found.

PATTERNITY

this year

and years later the echo

mirror, mirror

ghost pregnancy

ghost pregnancy

unwilling vessel at the
mercy of a dead thing

undesirable
kept for control

undesired
kept for convenience

a season for abandonment
traumatic anniversary

august & everyone
is dying

august & everything
is dying

what did i lose that day
what mother lost
what forestful of ancestors

my doppelganger
splits me from the hip

my doppelganger
tries to stitch our hips

together we are legion
turned against the self

ghost pregnancy

ghost pregnancy

abort, abort

sex is a desperate
survival

sex is a desperate
suicide

our generative love
will kill us sooner
than our sin

UNDERGROUND TWIN

when did i cut you off and bury you,
twin body dragged through the earth
beneath my feet. we're bound
by ties more pliable than muscle
and more permanent than bone.

remember why we tore
the ligaments that joined us,
you, my lateral translation,
mirror image, second throat
dirt-crammed and voice interred.

i can't remember our uncoupling
and panic—lose a whole year.
our thieves had no face and all faces.
i see thieves in every face i see.

//

the burning world flakes skin from me,
a trail of brown ash, chalking
outlines of your shadow below me.
i cannot reach you, phantom itch.

twin, did i bury you alive to keep
the thieves from taking both of us,
preserving us in hidden halves?

the rusted axe beside the bed
still seared into my flesh,
a hidden bruise.

our body is a scattering of cleaved parts.
i am starting to unmoor again
from memory. dear doppelganger,
do not let me bury myself too,
no matter how the coolness
of dark, wormy earth is poultice.

//

i feel you knocking knuckles
on the heard earth from below.
i feel my own against the concrete
as i signal back to you.

i slip into the grave they dug for us
to pull you out from underground,
rebirthing you from acid soil
greased like a newborn child
in shared blood, shit, and loam.

hold me so close we melt
back into one. let's join again,
a rage of hot unburial that burns
my bruises, galvanizes us, an alloy
soldering where we were cut.

GIFT

i.

child-sized, ungendered,
hidden under tables,
blanket forts, a secret
bigger than the hole
world. i was an initiate,
a novice sweaty-palmed,
ungenitaled until
the press of pink on pink.
you have to do it with us.
little hand i gave to pledge
plunged into pink fruit
of the loom, unready,
(never) tried to fight.

ii.

this time, fear, this time,
premature pubescence,
this time, boy hands
do not ask for invitation,
this time, breasts mean
readiness, this time, she looks
so much older, this time, locker
room talk, this time it burns,
fifth grade, hand, bra, this time
hot coals through clothes, *No*
this time, chanted, *No*, writhed

iii.

foresee the hatchet
by the bedside. death
threat. the rack of bones
foretelling what my body
was to be. i know i know
i should have known.
it suffocates and breaks.
dim gaslit body levitates,
gibbers in tongues
like Delphi's oracle

iv.

projection. this, the ritual
of protection: astral parts
thrust out of body.
it's a sacred art, sex
rendered ectoplasmic,
spools of cloth uncoiling
smoke-like from the mouth.
ours was a fabricated love
and i was false. across the bed
i left burnt poplar bark
and sifted yarrow seeds,
then left my body (it's a gift).

museum of reflective surfaces. glossed
black tiles, unnamed artists, crowd
insensate to the prickle of a stalked child,
ghost-reflected in glass cases of longing,
cold-sweat and glance over the shoulder,
conspicuous in a hall of telescopic lenses
when the crowd exhales a figure too familiar
pen-knifing my name into a placard—names me
into being, yokes displays of silence to my neck—
nausea of eye contact. how many faces
are his face, his beaked mouth snapping
toward my throat—tight anaphylactic,
choking sobs, pursuit unnoticed, the crowd
and its hover of wasps sucking grease
from anonymous art, untold authorship,

every lipless grin is his
                             & i collide

into a snaking warmth that grips my waist,
drags me through a frames, a painted maze,
barbed hedges, hawthorn woven to conceal
the boneless limb that leads me, umbilical
guide, taffy-pull of a girl in edwardian cotton,
white lace tourniquetting her headlessness,
neck a cut trunk scabbed and raw, pink ribbon
raises handlike where her lips should be
as *shhhhhh* she minotaurs us to the centre
of this pocket space, this thorn-walled haven
& my name dissolves behind us as my mouth
fills with saltspit and honey, tongue chewed free
unbloods itself mourning the sounds once used

to call ourselves. my mouth a leaking, sticky
hollow, teeth gone runny, egg-yolk gold,
my throat a funnel in pursuit of its own voice.

ZULA

some forms of care should not
be mutual   suicide watch,
don't hurt yourself i need you
not to let me hurt myself.

what a whiny brigade,   neighbour.
traipsing next door to pry
lit matches   heroin   knives
from your hands
                              couldn't heal
one of us,   nor could your kink
for other victims
                        i was endful
from fucking an addict who snuffed
theft   consent.   when he starved me
you offered a cigarette
                        all you could afford
the right kindness, wrong lungful

you   the alcoholic minister
who salvaged me,
                  but how
was i to tend your overdoses
once i started overeating
to destroy myself

                  we were hungry,
rotgutted,   together.
your cancer scare   expelled
in my lost pregnancy.

everyone thought we were fucking
when our nights were spent counting
our losses
                    our only touch
made in first aid,
                    harm reduction,

threatening   to call the cops
or hospitals   to lock each other up

                              knowing
we never could,   knowing
in spite of everything
                    like won't cure like.

BATSCRATCH

i eat my heavy loss
between the leakage
of the dream screech

rabid animal snarled
in my hair my sleep
my waking, ragged-
throated scream, torn
skin clawing the bastard
off my neck only—
no animal, only the rabbit
of arrhythmia against my ribs

& i unmoor for days

& bleed into another year
a long-since lover i expect
to find on waking, bone bruise
of an illness decades scarred,

a skittering across the ceiling
spectral rodents race
to strain cochlear bones—
tap tap tap beat phantom talons
in the walls, dry blood crusts
fingernails without a scratch
or scab or memory,

unfounded injury
unfounded crime

no blade or pinprick
but the needle of disease
between the eyes

APOCRITA

a long-haired jogger oozes through
the wall each night at five. fetch ouija!
gather roommates, open veil to ask
his name—electrostatic fuzz
and nothing more, our armhair feathered,
undrunk, party over. our benign guest
exorcized instead of welcomed?
nights unvisited
                              until the shock
of electricity booms in the kitchen.
blur of yellow in the dark. long oilskin
raincoat, sleeves dredging the floor.
impossible neck stretched taller
than upstairs neighbour's floor,
a blink, a hiss, the kitchen empty,
roommates staring, cold hands grasping
one another to be sure—
                              next night,
another in the hall.
                    two others faceless, arched
at open windows.
                    more loom above us
when we wake.
              we take turns hiding
on the fire escape, watch lightning
screech above, needled with hail,
wait out the visitors—
                       until the drum
of thunder cuts mid-beat.
                         & hail
suspends mid-fall, vibrating silent. inside,
tall demons rustle oilskins, gather in a circle.
the roommates gone. fresh seeping viscera

arranged in rhizomatic sigils on the ceiling,
a throb magnetic as a drooling void
yawns in the cigarette-burned rug—

& sound returns, a trypophilic groan
all timpani and hunger as all the tall ones bend
unending necks as though to drink, abyssal.

HYPNOGOGUE

bodiless hand in a violet glove
refracts the dreamer
& prismatic night.
time traveller, your night
mares galloping askance
in mirrors, cracked glass
dreamscope pressed
into your webbed eye.
a motherless mind
& a maelstrom. each night,
past & future collapse
in a silk glove, unwaking
cool sweat on the brow
& the fevered grasp of
violators—every touch
is *every* touch. is. every. touch.
turn back & unbecome. sleep
is no respite but a suicide
rehearsed. turn back
& take the gloved hand
of the night-rower in yours.

this is how to take the man out of complicity:
    killed backpacker ███ ████
    was into choking, bdsm

is fucking men at all
the darkest edge play
their conviction rate so low
that 99.5% just get off

last time i came
that many times
with any man
his bedside hatchet
dared my body

(tell me i enjoyed it)

pleasure is pleasure is please
stop is please stop is please

the heart wants
what wants blood

& this is how to tell a rape joke:

knock knock
who's there
    it's you, splitting in two
    headline / husk to fuck

hack hack

    that blunt blade by the bedside
  death threat / last breath

the heart wants
to want beating

look what you put inside yourself
		that bedside silicone
		dilators for the clench
		leather for pleasure is for please stop
		is for soft black cuffs to bind me
		to my body when it splits

what happens after the scene
is as important as the scene itself

& let me kink myself to death
		let me reclaim morality
		i mean mortality

survival is surfeit is surplus
is you should have died
if you knew what was best

(tell me i asked for it)

let none choose for me
when i choose to breathe

you can't consent to your own murder
but they'll ask if it was good for you

PRAYER TO SHUT THAT WHOLE THING DOWN

i.

to harvest myrrh for prayer

stigmata in tree bark
wound until the sap scabs
scrape the resin from the wounds
      refine and burn as offering

                / the same procedure succours to abort a virgin birth /

mortify the sinner's flesh, cut invocations in her skin
wash her in salt and holy water
scrape the resin from her womb
      the limp form she expels through steel mesh
      extrudes wet, purple crystals

ii.

when these crystals burn in prayer
the child will spring again
    pure,
    purged of bodyness

           and cleanse
           the sinner's loins

the child will speak a saviour's words

           o what a time / to be revived

iii.

now she burns
incense   for you

                                    now she burns
                    you   in effigy

iv.

do you feel pain
in your extremities   of virtue / of vice

pain   sermonizing
up your legs   such fire
you may never walk
                    / on water

                              do not

call for aid

                    this is no injury
                    no illness
                              but a warning

                              may you never

walk again

                              / toward

v.

we have read your prophet milton

       even satan has mixed feelings
       watching sin his daughter / wife
       grieving while tearing
       stem to stern to   forcebirth   for him

             hellhounds

                        clergy

          legal precedence

vi.

bless me
father / lover

i have sin

        -ged thy mantle

SLAPP / article ii

a thousand defamation suits playing at adam

naming us to death

renaming us
as corpses:

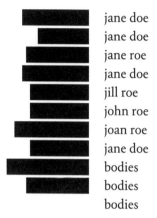

jane doe
jane doe
jane roe
jane doe
jill roe
john roe
joan roe
jane doe
bodies
bodies
bodies

how to hold a ▮▮▮▮▮▮▮▮ accountable
when bodies multiply
the ▮▮▮▮▮▮▮ vivisected

how to fight for ▮▮▮▮▮▮
with its last breaths labelled libel

// bind //

BITCHMEAT

blood in the teeth and dream
within a dream within a photograph.
the mounted bear head twinned
in yet another dreamer's selfie dump,
another name to flesh the tally—
& how many of us carry headless spirits
for the benefit of recognition, kinship,
since we cannot speak our names
to one another, nor the names
of hollow princes who have gripped
us by the jaw and whittled
their own likeness. when we meet
over a meal of sweetmeats, salt lard
on brioche, and morning gin, we laugh
about the family that may yet feed
upon our organs if we linger
in collusion. with dessert, we salt
the pet graves that were almost
our own graves, tally the bones
of our spent meal to cast a number,
ask how many others like us
occupy the space he carved
into our throats

PIECEMEAL

the wisdom teeth i never sent the warlock
safe-kept, spellcast in my pocket

little rashes run together, make a skin map.
landscape shifts across my face against all cortisones,
fruits over new ground, leaves a glacial trail cracked dry

an extra tooth grows from the bone arch of my left eye,
bone proscenium, bone curtain for the headache

joints hyperextend, pull taut to leave
a carcass they do not desire to constitute.
no balm, no relaxant,
no reason to stay so attached

eat only broth and rice two months against a poison,
allergy or botulism, pink balloon of putrefaction
cradled in the waistband, swelling
child imploding from your softest middle parts
and starving, stuffed with tar, and *starving*

covid exposure warning
contact 811 for testing

unearthly worms pass through your every pore
and orifice. excrete life forms that protest this eviction—
not even your muscles want inside you but the worms do

corneal infection, cataract inflection, crass incursion
of a mite of ash blown from the warlock's cigarette
across the water, sent to irritate, risk sight loss,
risk eye loss, secrete slime, threaten enucleation

twist-*POP* patellar dislocation
tendons jerked and cartilage made tear-able
to stop you running from his memory

another poison and the pains are hard to isolate:
which system screams over another
when this piecemeal thing disaggregates alone

but keep those broken teeth so close,
the only un-curse-nibbled talismans,
the permanence of bone shards pre-removed
all that remains inviolable

ANTHROPOCENE FETISH

apocalyptic hot nurse fantasy
clad only in a gas mask, matching
thong & bra. my cup size is 34ddt,
my crack a mariana trench
of climate change denial that gets
hotter, wetter, heavy-pets itself
to frenzy til we fry. what else
to do, when the only one coming
is species extinction. mutation
sprouts in the very depths

of my canal, wraps tendrils
around the inverted-cross IUD
that stops up all our future
generations. there's no question
of purity. our oncology,
i mean, ontology, grows rank
& pre-polluted in the womb.
spitters are quitters; let's be
swallowed in the swan song
of the sensory world.

i am a body unruly with love,
my sex a flaming tire fire
in the heat of meeting you.
put down your plastic cult,
i mean, your plastic cunt, & get
filthy. forget being green, clean,
& BPA-free. look, all this ripe,
organic goo we make as proof
we are so cultured.

put away your pyrrhic,
i mean, your empirical data,
& feel how language and i
go both ways. pick a safer word
than "big bang" for our gang bang
& get primal. extinction via meteor-
impact play is so last era;
now, we get our rocks off
from our own entropic cackle

i.

blonde revenant, you were exhumed for sale, for clickbait.
your name has been adopted by a cult who use your flame
for clout, for butts in seats on book tours shared with men
who rape women like us. the men who trolled our wrists
for papercuts, hospital bracelets, now tour the countryside
as feminists, bolstered by soldiers scripturing your voice.

ii.

rogue patroness of long-enduring, over-achieving, under-acknowledged
femmes, you cared for those you left. made sandwiches and sealed the
kitchen door. Though we learned from you to make provisions for the
victims of our suicidal days, you left no dogma for the harm we wish to
wreak as we flame out—in reciprocity against those who have harmed us,
those who watched, and those who laughed. Every october there are dime-
store sylvias in cheap blonde wigs and cardigans and cardboard ovens joked
over their heads. these bookish white girls think it's cute to dress their
boyfriends up as teddy, and to brush eyeshadow bruises on their arms.

iii.

saint of succour for bad mothers, for the birth-bound ones whose glow eclipses
children they love still, in spite of being consigned to birth them—
some are parents, who have mocked us for your worship, later selling you
for parts. when i miscarried, i had looked to them for comfort,
formulae for grief. when still i grieved i watched them bare their teeth
to grin with, not to bite back at the same men who de-mothered me.

iv.

at twenty-two i tried to die
and get back, back to you

but *peggy, peggy, you bastard, i'm through*
& s————, & a————, & l————,
& k————,   i'm through

v.

fulbright lady, we could burn ourselves like you. we longed to melt our
waxen bodies into acid when your voice was first commodified, then used to
dim our gaslit hearts. we are suicidal supplicants bearing the embryos that
bled out in our hands, the cast-off paperweights of men who trashed us.
there is a charge—if they will sell us, let them pay. do teach us how to die
and rise again, and how to burn away abuse, and how to reclaim our
appropriated prayers.

YOU MAY NEVER BE HEALTHY AGAIN

there was before the grounded lightning and now,
after / viral vectors swirl the clouds
the landscape altered / atomized

reach for them—jack pine sentinel and sprawling lake
/ shallow channel and blackwater deeps
/ rusted lily, reed, and heron
/ scents of pine and swamp gas / clean water and murk
/ summon phantom limbs to spider-weave / to snare the memory

you may never see these again.

/ no more homecomings
for the health / less /

ignite anise, firewood, pine sap
/ deplete hoarded stores / in divine isolation

recall your femme armour / queer laughter
/ found family in isolation three, four years
/ the trauma bonds that graft us at the cut
/ the choice to keep on living / still,
dark water / jack pines groaning in the wind

release the histories that bind new growth
/ brainwashing and abuse / immune suppression
/ mass pandemic / suicidal tendencies
/ ghost pregnancy / the CDC / MAiD
/ PTSD / false objectivity / new dis / ability

lay down the sting
of omnipresent death / threat

and release the voices you will not embrace
again / lost future loves / friends who abandon
/ suicidal drives / *i worry about you, little i—*

begin again /

PILLOW TALK

this marriage bed felt intimacy
fail me, twice. it watched me fuck
the third abuser almost with consent
& felt my body weighted, forced conception
of the mooncalf i would soon expel, dead
ripple of a child. absorbed my pleasure
and its last pearly emissions dried my husk
unfeeling in the nights cradled my limbs

that curdled into chicken feet, grew soft
walls and a roof, began to stalk away
upon new cloven hooves. we caught fire
in all the wrong ways. how does a phoenix
miscarry their own rebirth. no flaming
sex, no little gasp, only burnt earth.

zula, were you one of me or one of him
or both, like did he fuck you up
as bad as me or did he fuck you
just to see what it was like
to jerk around another predator.
i misjudged one and could have missed
you, too. so much for safe sex.
i was drunk in a fredericton alley
convinced i knew the two of you
like hands against my throat. remember
the month he left town & we careened
from a drag show, too triggered
by rape jokes, & drank on the bridge
& prank-called him, swigging jameson
from pocket flasks, hanging and howling
off the rotted railings they closed off
last year when one too many fools
like us fell off, or maybe jumped. remember
how he asked us both to marry him that night,
and how i wasn't sure when you agreed
if i was ever given any choice,
or who the first was to deny it.

TEMPERANCE, REVERSED

salt bath of my sweat
in a hospital gown. wake
as from drowning, the doctor
a single bright eye overnight
observation, still the swollen rot
flush in the womb. brace of needles
butterflied along both arms,
surgical tubing and the drip slow
drip of benadryl and sedative,
for your own good, velcro restraints
& hyperbaric throb & testing,
daily, for a cure:

tilt-table carousel to shake the sickness out

     diet of weight microaggressions

dry-tongued antidepressants

       homeopathic wasp sting, swarming hum

premature burial in salt and poplar ash

        strategic bone break of compression

scatter my torn limbs like the body of osiris

strapped in an antique wicker wheelchair
in this hall of mirrors, face distorts
unrecognizable,
                            doctors force-feed
oleander blooms, datura root,
collect my vomit in amber glass vials
to steep with rusted hobnails, grave dirt,
still no promise of a cure, hair wet,
lips fevered to be left alone, unhealed—

full butter moon on respite day.
skin antiseptic, scrubbed of evidence.

chaperone, walk me at dusk
to the flood, highway cordoned
for kayaks crossing downtown
in violet tides. dull-eyed companion,
find me any tide pool teeming
with a life unlike my own.

hard belly to the earth. my raw face
breaks the surface, cooled
by memory of freshet—eyes
gum open to a tv-static dance,
fervent mitosis, smoky organisms
swirl as drops of milk, quiver
as earthen hands form in bottom
of the flood to cup my cheek, glow
with my burning as their talons
mark the first cut on my brow.

RIVERSKIN

identify the land, the injury.
find water.
thank the generations who protect this.
hold your skin accountable to them.

etch spirals on a round stone offered by the river.
if the river offers no stones, wait a week.
a guide in swan's wings will bring seven stones; choose one.

the stone is mineral medium
imbedded in the flesh.

once granted invitation,
cast your stone into the water.
when the river spits silver esophagus
to hold your offering measure
the devil's throat, bright channel.
it will speak for you
the length of what you've lost.

skin will form upon the river's surface
as on scalded milk, a fine silk
you must gather, sew into a lantern
as it dries.

stitch with the hands of seven many-gendered kin.
one tells you of the new body she grows
inside her own. one smells of smoke and brings a book
of matches. one is young & still bears scabs
of your collective injuries.

together, hold the lantern high and light
a fire in its mouth. foam the river's surface
with your heat—a gift in thanks.

the lantern carries on the wind
and is enfolded,
then dissolves into itself.

to heal is to affirm the hurt and palm its stones,
to know the lantern will dowse out,
and not to need to wake it where it falls.

to heal is to allow rivers to cauterize
and to attend in mutual care.

every action has its counter.
every sunken stone a flight.
each weight a weightlessness.
each letting go a holding forth, an offering.

wait three more seasons for the flood.

CO-CONSTITUTED

my doppelganger keeps her stillborn,
does not flush it from her body like a virus.
she founds a sapphic commune, a village
of auncles to raise them—lets the stillborn
choose their name & gender once they speak,
& lets them learn to love their rot-pruned flesh.

never has a little aberration been so loved.
this half-human, half-chokecherry darling.

my doppelganger grants me visitation rights,
but I can tell she still laments her stillborn's
other half, the shrivelled twin that oozed
from my unreadiness, before her own.

her co-parents still disapprove, but can't deny
me & the stillborn were the same blood once
removed. the stillborn, their mother, & i
understand the removal of kinship,
the cervical ache of an unwanted thing
passing into the world pre-polluted.

when my own stillborn absorbed
into our flesh the killing curse
of their conception, that was sacrifice.
most mothering of arts.

how to mourn a phantom limb you never wanted.
how to shed a parasite you could have loved.

my doppelganger tells me our remaining child
has learnt to speak only in plurals. let us count,
little ones, starting with you.

HOTHOUSE

i. graft

conceal your sex
so well   so secret
it's forgettable

numb bulb withered
in a lockbox   clunky weight
to carry with you.
hear the rough sprig
clicking quietly inside.

you were told
this was all   you were told
this was all   you had to offer
              that offer you must.

that to be groped
was what you owe the world
to be allowed to live.
that this   is what you let
be done to you
to be worthy of love.

a gift pre-destined for another.
grown only to ripen
for the plucking

in the hothouse
there are razor blades
dangled above our heads   an offering
of self-harm to green-brown arms

never ask the cuttings
to consent to be transplanted
in another   never ask
the plant to take the graft.

ii. deflower

third grader overflowed
a c-cup   you're a woman now
and men will see you differently

child body   deflowerable
before you know the symbol
from the cut
          taught to fear
but not taught what to fear.

fear it all,   overachiever.

won't somebody save the children

      keep the children's hands

           above their blankets
           lest they know how to object

iii. root rot

how to choose
your first   (chosen) undoing.

hide our post-pubescent bodies
from our parents   hide
the condoms from our parents
hide our mutual   irradiance.

failed to love you without fearing
failed to love the cancer   (me)
failed to give a self to you i didn't have.

we deepened root rot
in my body as we built
what clumsy gorgeous little sex
we could

had i known how to love you
i would.   and not this mimicry,
                coercions of a self.

iv. buy me flowers

how to trust my secret flower
when we are euphemisms
only   and are cut down
by the dozen   sold for profit
bought by men
as half-assed compensation   for harms done.

a posy   for a blowjob
                and forgiving

roses   for regretting getting bruises
                on your face

daisies   for the damage
                to your soft, internal folds
                a scar so deep you bury it   in blossoms.

a dying dozen sorries   fresh bouquet
of plantly genitals snipped
for his fancy.
                he once told me
he couldn't buy me flowers
or the secret could disperse
secret   he made me
                                to protect
himself

he left
        a spray
                of plastic flowers on the bed

of blood and cum
across my face

                undead reminders.

v. hothouse

in the hothouse we are suicidal,
wax-leafed things   and grow
carnivorous   and feast upon
our own green flesh
for lack of sustenance.

you have dug your tendril teeth
into your own bitter brown arms.

you have tried to re-graft
where your nerves were cut

we are unfed   undead orchids
plucked by wanton fingers.
we are undone by revenges
etched   in scar tissue
and root rot that we spread
amongst ourselves.

in the hothouse, razor blades
and eggshells cut our soil.

when we cleave   ourselves
we cauterize   to heal.

new pandemic, and a porous thing flies westward
to sakura blooms impatient in the bud,
itching to burst. a suitcase rattling with tarot,
steroids, vitamins, and herbs. a body barely cauterized,
and hypopigmented where weeks ago cracks oozed.

here lies a cross-coast convalescent wrapped
in cold cotton for skin rash, full-body eruption.
soaked in premature sun, afterbirth of birdsong.
must a person fly this far during the harshest warming,
covid-19 warnings, just to heal?

scarified fireweeds sprout from the left knee.
that highway-ditch death bloom breaks skin
and leaves me yet more open to contagion.
reckless, buoyant with a second course of prednisone,
and made defenceless by that medicine that keeps the eyes
and throat from clamping access shut—

                    i am compromised

biding long hours in an isolated lightscape,
phototherapy, a loft bed where the moon beckons,
skin charged magnetic with its tidal swell and slough.

pull a knight of pentacles, non-binary, and backlit
by the rising sun. they sprout two stag-horn ferns
from outstretched, driftwood arms. this garden love
too distant when the cardinal directions cease to mean,
and viral vectors bloom and isolate—

                    let us someday call this over-caution.

guide a body home and painless like an anxious lover
hesitates, their saltworn hands a soft remittance.

queer knight, tend your quarantine garden
until the bleak wind blows this skin-shell back
to consummate our cracked embrace. with bladderwrack
and aloe,
          let us cleanse the wounds we keep.

carmen and i bring molten spruce boughs
to the shell of the abandoned church,
adorning crook and crevice with the frizz
of withered branch. i lay my tarot on the altar
where the catholics once broke bread,
light six candles the colour of brown flesh
to dispel the ghosts of every piece of bread
turned god-flesh, chewed to mush.

maria comes to say the river has broken
its water—it follows her in. i draw five cards
around the wet curve of her pregnant belly,
pushed against the altar, swollen harvest moon.
the water reaches us too soon, drowns
candles as carmen takes our hands to run,
leaving our ritual unread, unheeded.

from higher ground we watch the church swept
to the center of a trash-infested lake
that once was forest, home. crushed plastic
bottles bobbing in our wake. how to admit
we are a self-despoiling ecosystem, suicidal
network. every flood a purgative collapse.

carmen and i construct a makeshift raft
around our bodies where we stand.
maria says we'll need new magics
as this world ends—kill your darlings,
your familiars. together, as we float,
we ask the water how to want
to keep on living for each other
when we sink.

HOW TO TRANSUBSTANTIATE

thank the scrap dolls refruiting dead trees
on an island, mid-river. the limbs the dolls
drop, like overripe drupes leaking nectar,
will constitute your parts. first, ask permission
of the ghost girl mothering their island; every
virgin worth her worship commands power.
for a dear price, she will furnish your eyes
with hand-painted clay beads from the sockets
of her first doll, the cloth-and-straw daughter
she drowned for, to save from the river.
be thankful for these. you are bodily, wanting.

//

next, move south. find the wild gods
and lay yourself down to be sculpted
by plantain-branch arms, by warm palms
like broad kapok leaves fanned over canopies,
hogging the sunlight. these gods carve
a dense crown on your ramshackle skull,
cut a ring of stone curls to protect you.
these are giving gods, and will not scant
their care on guests bearing no harm.
they salt the colour of your skin
with a pre-glottal stop in their language,
that language like mud underfoot,
each syllable a bare sole sinking into
sun-warmed earth. they will crimson your lips
with the lick of divine, wine-pink tongues
as they lavish their river-bank scriptures
upon you. here, learn how to be gentle.
learn how to be held and to hold in return.

//

go now and find the western idols frozen
in enamel. teach them to recite with you
the mineral namesakes that burnish
your brows, to sing deep in the throat
where the colour of your skin was created.
let this likeness arouse a new faith
in these brillo-pad virgins. allow them
to offer their sanitized names to the trees,
pray for diphthongs. bewitch them to exit
their pale iron frames. let them dance,
clad in coarse linen tunics with thin bows
they weave from dried papaya rinds. together,
remove your brown hands from the worship
of stone vaults, of chapels carved deep
in the salt mines, of mining itself. return
to worshipping the salt and bathe together
in its waters. let it marinate your bodies
in advance of the devouring of your flesh.

in cyprus, when a fig seed feeds on what it fed
it roots the body of a murdered man,
his stomach sprouting to the light.
Ahmet is found after thirty-seven years,
a half-life. return the fruits he bears
back to his kin.

signal the synecdoche of me
scattered across the country in the beds
where you winnowed my phantom limbs.
i am dead meat. opportunistic omnivore,
i cannot grow my body back to light.
sustained only by scraps, no wonder
i dissociate so freely, coming off the bone
like any scavenged carcass—you, the alpha
predator who road-killed me then tenderized,
spit-lubricated me.
                              i long for something green
to keep me whole. for want of fruit,
my severed parts ooze fleshy tendrils
from their bloodstains, saturate the ground
i no longer can walk with little, grey-brown
feelers, flashing spores to locate one
another.
                  i will web my dead limbs back
together below ground.
                                    what you killed
in me will mushroom, clouding underfoot.

you never finished what you started.
some of us die so alive our corpses
grow to feed erotic flora. Ahmet

and his fig tree bear seedy, brown fruits
that draw in wasps to crush, grind
into sweet meal, his death a honey death
that keeps on giving.   the parts you killed
in me grow ghostly, neither flesh nor fruit,
fed on electrochemistry, on memory,
on cures for retrograde amnesia.

we have reconnected since you left us
less than corpse. our preternatural growth
makes us the largest organism in this earth,
our haunting larger than your violations.
we grow hungry.

SLAPP / article iii

████████████████   speech is free
only to those who can afford to ████████
the brace of custom leather muzzles
fitted to the mouths
they forced & tore

████ scold's bridle ████████████████
                    too little
                    too legal
                    too tight

on the face
                    bleached white leather cuts
into the cheeks   reflects ████████
in the numb cataracts of the eyes

            ████████ sick white glow
the eyes weep their own jelly   in protest

laborious pull of a stillbirth in ████████
            tectonic   ache
against these forced extractions

what more
can they take
                    who have plundered scraped wombs

what more
can they take
                    who have taken us ████████████

what more
can they take
                    who have killed ████████
                    & claimed victimhood

what good is a rape shield in a death match

hollow shell against our naming
that dissolves in █████ precedence

// devour //

CABRA NEGRA

la cabra aparece y me sigue insistiendo
que empieze los ritos. compels me to obey,
has me now sleepless for a fortnight
foraging for ground cherries, red fruit
now overflows my bathtub, preparation
for the ritual he demands, my bare feet
stained with berry juice and earth,
fearing his hooves will break my feet
if once i hesitate—days, when he sleeps,
i comb his long black fur, wind braids
around his horns, his musky scent
like charred hay sticking to my skin—

one night while gathering i jump across
the creek and visit home, where mother
sleepwalks, washes out my hair
with holy water from a vial she kept
inside her ruana, wraps me in her arms
to whisper comfort, then floats to bed
to sleep, no memory of my return—

la cabra no me mira cuando llego,
empezando ya los ritos, burrowed
in the spilling mound of berries
as i add my last night's findings,
oozing wine across the floor under his weight,
he begs me to begin—cut kindling
for the fire, so i heave the axe and strike
into the hearthwood, feel a splash
then see my hair has bound itself
around my wrists and guided me to strike
into his skull—warm spray across my face
la sangre de la cabra y su grito animal,

my hair withers and breaks as the axe
pierces his skull and i awake and panic,
ritual ruined or changed, strange song
buzzing the bones of my forearms—

& where to hide this evidence? the neighbours
have a garden, fresh-turned earth,
but how to risk their knowing, blood
and fruit staining my skin, the smell
of rust and rotting berries at my feet—

i grip the axe's bladed head and draw
against his spine, peel off his hide
and smash his hooves, mash berries
into meat and eat his innards, feed
myself fresh meat into the morning
when the dew condenses in my hair,
i scrape his hide and clothe myself.
sever the left horn from his empty skull
and hollow it to sing through.

IUD/IED

i. explosively formed penetrator

femme thin-armoured
& cannibal, desertic body
planting the husk of our child
on the trail where he ashed
cigarettes before staking
my flesh from below
upskirt harpoon

                         emergency measures
                         peck peck   bird beak
                         forced through the cervix
                         for insertion

spraying sons he dreamed of
at our feet   stab stab
since what is more insurgent
than a white man denied
entry   blazing past frontiers
wet shrapnel spatters
endometrium & lodges
to grow   fester

                         expulsion an ache in reverse
                         not a birth but rejection embodied
                         a cursed, curdled thing   slips
                         between muddied thighs

ii. victim-operated

femme a ticking time bomb
friendly-fire friendzone
triggered bitch is asking
for it, triggered   playing victim

> VOIED as victim-operated
> improvised explosive device
> VOIED as   *designed to function*
> *upon contact with a victim*

a femme with a womb
is a resource   extractable
gaslight the fuse, throw
a life in her   de-flower
de-roe-v-wade her

> beware, male artists: emptiness
> does not belong to you
> femmes *are* the VOID

iii. switch (activator)

femme turned weapon
against the child he trashed in me
this appetite   hostile unmother

          this revenge body: mutated goldfish
          birthed and flushed
                   or
          baby weight.   half ton
          of dirty matter he's not touched

i shred green seed husks to desiccate
our bloodroot baby   feed
its juices to my scaffolding
and let a bitch grow   stronger

unmother, vampire,   suckles life
from her castaway sons.   cackles,
paints amniotic fluid like a face mask.
self care for the care-worn

          plan c   copper coil or progestin
          make the self hostile, acidic
          a cervix armed with plastic teeth
          string tips dangle
                stab stab motherfucker

iv. conventional weapons

sanctioned missile manufacture
genocide the global south
noble deaths   so *heroic*
to make room for preborn whites

> *sharp pain in the chest*   *crushing chest pain*
> or heaviness   heart attack   swelling
> in the calf   stroke   loss
> of vision   breast cancer diabetes
> ectopic pregnancy   pid   cysts on the ovary
> uterine perforations   perforations   perforations

no defense for brown femmes
fighting just to live   fighting

                   don't ask
don't tell us this is war   your rape
is baptism by fire   a right, we mean,
a rite of passage   holy war

> ptsd is a soldier's disease is a man's world
> is screaming   unsoldier   unman
>   unbitch   unwoman
> unmother   unnatural will—
>
> all terror to the femme body unterrorism
> unterror   unterror

v. improvise

if this body must teem
new cell growth   let it sprout
cankers in the womb
              to transplant into men
who planted violence in us

                    harvest our own seed not to grow
                    in blasted soil   but to be boiled,
                        distill   abortifacient salves
                    poultice against the harms of weapons
                    femme was forced to be

& improvise a new unmaking of our own.
& let them bear explosive charges
for a change.

                    if we must be triggered
                    let us blast holy oblivion.

                    if we must be unnatural
                    unliving   monstrous
                    let us feed

dress code infraction of my body
silhouetted, awkward, overgrown
against a *save the children* billboard.

never tell the children what was done
to us already.

              queer ancestress,
brown paper doll torn into convent
schools across los andes, pray for us,
antepasada, to la virgen del carmen
to spare us her future.

                  let us not
be known for silence taught us
by our fathers.
              let our bodies never
line the gilt floors of school chapels
to be trodden on by men who claimed
our childhoods as communion
to be spilled.
             let us desanctify
the ancestry of theft that replicates
all genders known only
as violable.

           déjanos resplandecientes
y sin género, ungenitaled as children,
fill us beyond all borders
                with a dream-
less future

as we choose—yes—
let us sleep—yes—unmolested
by the hounds—yes,

let none choose
for us how we choose to breathe

we brought our doppelgangers to the gang bang,
let them rest their heads against the other's breasts
to suckle comfort. our trouble is we need
doubles to teach us to love one another. we need
collective heat to heed our own desires. we each split
at the hilt—you & your twin are mythic when you spread
your youth between us with an effervescent ease.
erotic charge of elasticity. your skin's clean smell
of garlic, spiced squash, forest frost—i taste
new leather in my mouth. my double chokes
with hunger, pleasure. she & i know how it feels
to keen before the injury. we crave the thunderclap
of your collective hands
                              and when we come
home late-night roiling, metamour, you and your echo
both are present by residual scent. your phantom
limbs bow notes augmenting our continued minuet
as thunder underscores the rain. we're drunk
on ozone flash, the lightning's gasp

THE GENDER TODAY IS A SPLIT PLUM & DAD BOD

become a gender like a promised mouthful,
hungry gut unreproductive as an asset,
like you never knew your dry wit, your fluidity,
your soft contours could be a stone fruit splitting,
that androgyny and transformation are both
orifice and armour. semi-porous skin shapeshifts—
and what a revelation! and what an electric
plum orange, bright flesh oozing over dark
skin. what abundance! moon-tits willendorf
with butch-punch arms, slick body syruped
into plush hips, lush licks. gender soft- and hard-
ens into questions, pleasure in the asking—
is this good for you? how do you want it
today? rough? with spit? with elation?
and always relation. a thick-plum femme
tops loosened terms, my sweet meat pressed
and oozing down your wrist—let me daddy-
bottom, be a vulnerable father, sweet
and open and most giving. let me feed you
this ripe question of a body. swallow with me
all the soil and shit i've grown through
to burst full and tart against your tongue.

THE HORSES ARE A METAPHOR FOR WOMEN I HAVE BROKEN,

said the mentor in his poems, except
the poems admitted this in spite of him.
his horses came to us as nightmares,
heads bowed to conceal the shock
of our own faces which he painted
over theirs. like mirror images, rough
brow to brow, we stood and grieved
together for the fucked-up centaurs
we were forced to be, our bodies
trading memory by touch. after
the nightmares came the ships,

the nameless vessels he poured out
into his poems to stake unasked claim
over the body of the sea, conquistador
uncaring for his casualties. the ships
asked us to count the mingled bloods
that stained their masts—how many
bodies harpooned, left to wither
into sails—how many strands of hair,
our hair, were woven into sails to stop
the wind—how many names spilled
over the storm decks and erased. then,

from the water, we were undrowned
by the vultures. in a brace of bone
that once bore feathers, we set down
on land to hear them ask forgiveness:
fleshless birds that once in taxidermy
loomed above his bed and watched him
break us, now repenting how they tore
our meat to re-member their own. how
to begrudge the scavengers the flesh

that they were tossed, though it was ours.
they offer us their bones to build anew

prosthetic limbs, to join our old bones
into theirs into each other—we become
another form, a multitude, a gryphon
multiplied, a fractal rooted in the mud
where we were buried, bone stems
softening and blooming up like fungi,
a parasite asking consent to join the body
of each new host we encounter, joining
horse and tree and ship and creek,
survivors, every-gendered, joining bodies
joining limbs with every body human,
more than human, every body that
was ever used as poetry by rapists.

scar tissue cushions every joint
of vulture bone and painted face,
survivor skill etched in each whorl
of fur or fingertip. we soften
into weapon—we protect ourselves.
we stand for nothing
but ourselves inside this poem.

SLAPP / dissolution

justice is the final score they make of us
the wasted ▮▮▮▮▮▮ memorial
too little
too larval
too late

justice is a woman chopped
& sued by her attacker

justice is a many-gendered war
a ▮▮▮ forgetting

justice is

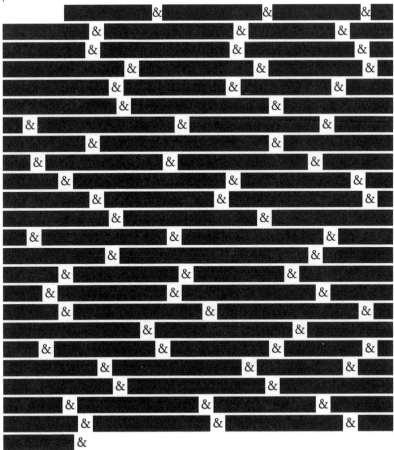

// ACKNOWLEDGEMENTS //

More gratitude than I can express is owed to Canisia Lubrin, Kelly Joseph, and the M&S crew for helping this book find its form. This book required more trust than I knew I could find, and you gave it. Thanks to Talia Abramson for all the evolutions of the cover art (all of them!). Thank you to Billy-Ray and Eli for holding these poems, and for the liberatory art you make.

Many poems in this collection have appeared in previous incarnations, with thanks to the editors and readers who gave them space. Thanks to Mallory Tater and Rahila's Ghost Press; to the jury of the 2019 Bronwen Wallace Award for Emerging Writers; to Marilyn Dumont and Rob Taylor for their respective editions of *Best Canadian Poetry*; to Ian LeTourneau of Emergency Flash Mob Press; to Annick MacAskill of Opaat Press; and to the editors of *Arc*, *CV2*, *The Ex-Puritan*, *GUTS*, *Poetry is Dead*, and *Room*.

An earlier version of this manuscript was supervised during my Ph.D. by Triny Finlay and Randall Martin, who I cannot thank enough for their support. Much gratitude to the writer kin who keep me grounded: Emily Skov-Nielsen, Katie Fewster-Yan, Claire Kelly, Ambrose Albert, Lauren Turner, Brendan Vidito, Colin Johnson, Lauren Korn, Patrick O'Reilly, Lisa Banks, Liz Howard, Natalie Wee, & all the Banff loves.

To my chosen families and covens, for the tarot readings, tea adventures, hospital visits, and belly-laughs through hell: Daniel, Maggie, Róisín, Joan, Amber, Reid, Indigo, Siobhán, Melanie, Mario, los Salazar, y los Leon. To all my queer, trans, mad, disabled, migrant, racialized, abolitionist, anti-colonial, pro-liberation kin: you are every possible future.

Lastly, this book would not exist without the unnameable networks of survivors who keep one another as safe as we can through the silencing, the rage, the grief, and the monstrosity of what we are made out to be. I would not be alive without you. Another world is possible, and it begins with I believe you, I believe you, I believe you.

Many of the poems in this collection quote directly or adapt material from other authors. My thanks to the authors and their publishers for the permission to reprint their words, and often, for saying what I could not.

"witch hunt" is written after and in conversation with Lauren Turner's "Can I still be an emerging female writer if I don't know tarot?" originally published in *Peach Mag*.

"exquisite corpse" is a cento composed of lines from books I read during the 2019 Sealey Challenge, originated by Nicole Sealey. Following the order in which they appear in the poem, each line is excerpted from the following:

Virginia Konchan's "The New Alphabets" in *The New Alphabets* (Anstruther Press, 2019); Natalie Diaz's "As a consequence of my brother stealing all the lightbulbs" in *When My Brother Was an Aztec* (Copper Canyon Press, 2012); Lauren Turner's "Stop Bringing Me Here" in *The Only Card in a Deck of Knives* (Wolsak & Wynn, 2020); Ivanna Baranova's "Confirmation Bias" in *Confirmation Bias* (Metatron Press, 2019); Nancy Lee's "Chronic" in *What Hurts Going Down* (McClelland & Stewart, 2020); Dani Couture's "The Omega Trick" in *Black Sea Nettle* (Anstruther Press, 2016); Rasiqra Revulva's "Free the Niqabi!" in *Cephalopography 2.0* (Wolsak & Wynn, 2020); Domenica Martinello's "Parthenope, Embodied" in *All Day I Dream of Sirens* (Coach House Books, 2019); Danez Smith's "my bitch!" in *Homie* (Graywolf Press, 2020); Jaclyn Desforges' "It's the Small Things That Save Us" in *Hello Nice Man* (Anstruther Press, 2019); Nisa Malli's "Anaphylaxis" in *Remitting* (baseline press, 2019); Chen Chen's "Kafka's Axe & Michael's Vest" in *When I grow up I want to be a list of further possibilities* (BOA Editions, 2016); Brooke Carter's "Dead Girls Don't" in *Poco Loco* (Anstruther Press, 2016); Shazia Hafiz Ramji's "Gerrid" in *Prosopopoeia* (Anstruther Press, 2017); David Ly's "Mythical Man (II)" in *Mythical Man* (Palimpsest Press,

2020); Rebecca Rustin's "Backlog" in *Mercy Tax* (Rahila's Ghost Press, 2019); Cara Nelissen's "Fragmentation, IV" in *Pray For Us Girls* (Rahila's Ghost Press, 2019); Kyla Jamieson's "Future Body Self Portrait" in *Kind of Animal* (Rahila's Ghost Press, 2019); the line "but the body (little bitch) won't love you back" is excerpted from Robin Richardson's *Sit How You Want* published by Signal Editions/ Véhicule Press in 2018, by permission of the author and the publisher; Ocean Vuong's "Headfirst" in *Night Sky with Exit Wounds* (Copper Canyon Press, 2016); Phoebe Wang's "Still life with raw carcass, shallots and small comforts" in *Room 43.2* (*Room* magazine, 2020); torrin a. greathouse's "To the People Who Call Me Brave" in *There Is a Case That I Am* (Damaged Goods Press, 2017); Stevie Howell's "Dew" in *Summer* (Desert Pets Press, 2016); Michael Prior's "My Father's Birthday is the Day Before Mine" in *Burning Province* (McClelland & Stewart, 2020); Tracy K. Smith's "Interrogative" in *duende* (Graywolf Press, 2007); Estlin McPhee's "why I love boy bands" in *Shape Shifters* (Rahila's Ghost Press, 2018); Nolan Natasha's "From God" in *I Can Hear You, Can You Hear Me?* (Invisible Books, 2019); Brandi Bird's "Eat Your Elders" in *I Am Still Too Much* (Rahila's Ghost Press, 2019); Natalie Diaz's "These Hands, If Not Gods" in *Postcolonial Love Poem* (Graywolf Press, 2020); Joe Jiménez's "If only my arms could offer fruit, let the sun be called—" in *Pulse/ Pulso: In remembrance of Orlando* (Damaged Goods Press, 2018); and torrin a. greathouse's "Who Is Monster" in *boy/girl/ghost* (TAR Chapbook Series, 2018).

The italicized lines and statistics in "little deaths" are excerpted from the following: the headline from an article by Lee Brown about the 2018 murder of Grace Millane in the *NY Post*; statistics compiled by RAINN ("out of every 1000 sexual assaults, 995 perpetrators will walk free."); Amber Dawn's essay "Cunts & Catastrophes: Trauma Play and Writing" in *The Rumpus*; and comments from Brian Dickey, prosecutor in the case against the man who killed Grace Millane, as quoted by Anna North in an article in *Vox*.

"piecemeal" borrows its title and, loosely, its conceit from an episode of the same name in Jonathan Sims' podcast *The Magnus Archives*.

Several lines in "anthropocene fetish" are adapted from or directly excerpted from David Abram's *The Spell of the Sensuous: Perception and Language in a More-Than-Human World* (Vintage Books, 2012) ("Meaning sprouts in the very depths of the sensory world, in the heat of meeting, encounter, participation"); and a blog entry by author Cary Fagan reviewing my own chapbook, *Guzzle* ("Reading *Guzzle* I feel as if I've been touched all over by hands sticky with some ripe organic goo, sometimes stroked, sometimes tickled, sometimes slapped").

Parts iv. and v. of "selling lady lazarus" borrow lines and language from Sylvia Plath's "Daddy" and "Lady Lazarus," from *Ariel* (Faber and Faber Ltd, 1965). The italicized line in part iv. is from a tweet by Adèle Barclay.

The italicized line in "you may never be healthy again" is from a conversation with Cecily Nicholson, who read and advised me on an early excerpt from this manuscript after we were connected through the Bronwen Wallace Award for Emerging Writers. My thanks to Cecily for her wisdom.

"IUD/IED" includes lines adopted or adapted the Wikipedia page on Improvised Explosive Devices; Audrey Wollen's "Girls own the void" meme; and the "Risks of Using MIRENA" section of the product monograph issued by Bayer for the Mirena IUD.

"the gender today is a split plum & dad bod" is a riff on the @genderoftheday Twitter bot created by Misha Fletcher.

REBECCA SALAZAR (she/they) is a queer, disabled, and racialized Latinx writer currently living on the unceded territory of the Wolastoqiyik people. Their first full-length collection *sulphurtongue* (McClelland & Stewart) was a finalist for the Governor General's Award for Poetry, the New Brunswick Book Awards, the Atlantic Book Awards, and the League of Canadian Poets' Pat Lowther Memorial Award.